WEMBLEY 2

 129 YEARS IN THE WAITING

First published in Great Britain in 2008 by
The Breedon Books Publishing Company Limited
Breedon House, 3 The Parker Centre,
Derby, DE21 4SZ.

ISBN: 978-1-85983-672-9

Printed and bound by Progress Press, Malta.

WEMBLEY 2008

129 YEARS IN THE WAITING

Steve Uttley, Kate Evans and Phil Ryan   **Text by Tony Bluff**

Special thanks to Dave Richards, Suzanne Uttley, Barry Watson, Press Association and the Supporters for their photographic contributions.

breedon **books**
PUBLISHING

McCammon 71), Mark Wilson, Richie Wellens, Martin Woods (Sean McDaid 84); James Hayter (Lewis Guy 77), Paul Heffernan. Three days later, the same players turned out against League Two side Lincoln City in the first round of the Carling Cup, at the Keepmoat Stadium, with Lincoln going back home defeated comprehensively by four goals to one. Hayter scored his first competitive goal for the club in the first half, with Wellens following suit and Heffernan and McCammon also registering on the score sheet in the second half. While this result was welcomed, Sean O'Driscoll reiterated that the club's main ambition was to win promotion to the Championship. Expecting this result to kick-start the season, there was disappointment ahead as the next three games were lost, two in the League, at Hartlepool United (1–2) and at home to Bournemouth (1–2), and a League Cup match at Plymouth Argyle (0–2). The same starting line up played in the two League games, but before the game against Hartlepool Matt Mills, a 21-year-old centre-half who had played under Sean O'Driscoll at Bournemouth two years earlier, had been signed on loan from Manchester City. He made his debut when he came on as a substitute for Gareth Roberts against Bournemouth, but Rovers lost the game which meant they dropped to 20th in the table. The starting line up at Plymouth showed three changes: Matt Mills for Gordon Greer, Sean McDaid for Mark Wilson and Lewis Guy for James Coppinger, who had torn an ankle ligament against Bournemouth, but Plymouth proved to be far superior, winning comfortably in the end.

Changes were made to the side for their visit to Swansea City on the first day of September. Brian Stock came in for his first game of the season after a hernia operation and replaced Martin Woods, Gordon Greer was brought in for Lewis Guy to provide a five-man back line, Mark Wilson replaced Sean McDaid and Mark McCammon was preferred to Paul Heffernan up front. At this

stage of the season there were few signs of what was to come from Swansea, but the Rovers played well enough to come away with their first win of the season, showing what could lie ahead for them. Wellens scored a couple of goals in the last quarter of the game after Bodde had been sent off just past the hour for a head butt on Stock, and the win lifted the Rovers to 13th place. A Johnstone's Paint Trophy goal feast from the Rovers mid-week buried Bradford City at the Keepmoat, with five goals shared by McCammon, with two, Guy, Woods and a Harban own-goal, as Bradford could only muster one goal in reply. This was achieved despite making six changes to the starting line up from the Swansea game, as the manager utilised the resources at his disposal.

A Friday night visit to Northampton Town on 7 September saw the Rovers going down by two clear goals to give the Cobblers their first victory of the season. The manager had reverted to the line up that started the game at Swansea, but it wasn't to be the Rovers' night, mainly due to the performance by the Northampton goalkeeper, Mark Bunn, who was named Man of the Match for an outstanding display.

After playing on a Friday because of an England game on the Saturday, Rovers' next game was on a Sunday because of the St Leger meeting the day before. This match against Crewe Alexandra at the Keepmoat Stadium saw Gordon Greer replaced by Lewis Guy in a tactical change and Paul Heffernan came in for the injured Mark McCammon. The Rovers won comfortably, with goals from Heffernan in the first half and an own- goal by Danny Woodards in the second. The following week's match was at Southend United, who had come down the previous season from the Championship and were already battling for the Play-off places. Another tactical move brought Gordon Greer in for James Hayter, who dropped to the bench. The match was played on a sunny day, and Rovers had gone in at half-time leading

2–1, after going 1–0 down on 25 minutes, but taking the lead with goals from Gareth Roberts, with a free-kick from 30 yards, and Lewis Guy. However, in the first 15 minutes of the second half the home team stormed the Rovers goal and rattled in a couple from Alan McCormack and Leon Clarke to put them in the lead, which they managed to hold to the final whistle. A win at home to lowly Cheltenham Town on the last Saturday of September, courtesy of goals in each half from Guy and Mills, left the Rovers in 10th place at the end of the month.

A mid-week visit from bottom club Walsall saw the visitors leave the Keepmoat with all three points from a 3–2 win. The Rovers made one enforced change, Sean McDaid coming in for Gareth Roberts, who had a groin strain, and one tactical change, with Gordon Greer being replaced by James Hayter. In a game of two halves, to quote an old cliché, the Rovers won the first half so easily that it is a wonder how they had failed to go in at the break leading by four or five goals. Mills and Guy had got their names on the score sheet for the second week running to give them a 2–1 lead. The fans were asking each other how many the Rovers would get in the second half, but in the end it was a different story as Walsall took the game by the scruff of the neck from the off. Halfway through the half Walsall levelled the score and then went in front four minutes later after being awarded a penalty. The Rovers tried to hit back and were given a penalty in the 90th minute, but Coppinger dragged it wide. To make matters worse, Guy apparently spoke out of turn to the referee and was despatched to the dressing room. This result seemed to have an effect on the team because it heralded a run of 10 unbeaten games which took them to the fringe of the Play-off positions, starting with a 1–1 draw at Luton Town on Saturday 6 October, with Hayter scoring in the first half and the home team in the second. A game in the Johnstone's Paint Trophy against Oldham Athletic had been scheduled for the following

Tuesday at the Keepmoat, but because Oldham had three players on international duty it was postponed until the 23rd. On the Sunday, Huddersfield Town came to the Keepmoat in a televised match on Sky Sports and were beaten by two goals, one from Stock after 13 minutes and another from Wilson on 65 minutes. Gordon Greer had replaced Steve Roberts, who had suffered an ankle injury at Luton, and the same team lined up at the City Ground the following Saturday in a fiercely contested goalless draw against high-flying Nottingham Forest. The following Tuesday the Johnstone's Paint Trophy second-round game against Oldham Athletic was played at the Keepmoat, with the Rovers making four changes to the squad. Oldham played their strongest team and were soundly beaten by three clear goals, all scored in the second half, by Price, Green and Woods. The last Sunday in October brought League leaders Leyton Orient to the Keepmoat. An even first half left the score sheet blank, but the second half was as different again. Jason Price replaced Sean McDaid after the break and put the Rovers in front seven minutes into the half. Orient hit back four minutes later and then took the lead halfway through the half. This time the Rovers hit back within two minutes through Price to level the score, and eight minutes from time Hayter executed a brilliant overhead kick to put the Rovers in front. Wellens wrapped it up two minutes from time, and the Rovers ended October in 11th place in the table.

The Rovers took to the road for the first two weeks in November, playing four away games on the trot. First up was a trip to Swindon Town, resulting in another three points with goals from Stock and Guy, one in each half. This was followed by a trek to Gillingham, where a Hayter penalty midway through the second half salvaged a point. The following Saturday it was FA Cup first-round day and a short journey over the Pennines to play Oldham Athletic. They were two goals down after 49 minutes but battled back to parity, with goals from Hayter after 63 and 86 minutes. Finally, a trip to Grimsby Town in the Johnstone's Paint Trophy quarter-final proved unlucky. The Rovers made seven changes to the team from the Oldham game. Grimsby took an early lead but Guy equalised halfway through the first half. Then, two minutes before the interval, a back header by Mills to Smith was carried by the strong wind over the 'keeper and into the net to give the home team the lead. Although the Rovers dominated the second half, it was 11 minutes from time before they equalised with a penalty from Heffernan. With the scores level after 90 minutes, the match moved straight to penalties. Green had the first penalty saved, but Wilson, Heffernan, Wellens and Greer scored theirs. Grimsby scored their first four penalties, with one penalty to take to win the match. Smith saved the kick from Bolland, but to Grimsby's delight the referee ordered a re-take for encroachment. This time Bolland made no mistake and the team in the semi-final was Grimsby Town. Was defeat a good thing for the Rovers? Grimsby Town went on to Wembley but lost to Milton Keynes Dons. The Rovers could have gone on to win it again, but their pursuit of promotion may well have suffered. During the majority of penalty kicks you see encroachment, but re-takes are rarely given, so perhaps the referee, in hindsight, did the Rovers a favour. We shall never know.

The following Saturday a goalless draw ensued against Tranmere Rovers at the Keepmoat. A sterile first half was followed by the sending off of Carl Tremarco for a bad tackle on Wellens two minutes into the second half, but even against 10 men the Rovers could not break through the Tranmere defence. However, the following Saturday the Rovers returned to winning ways when they went to Port Vale with virtually the same personnel. They scored a convincing 3–1 win over the next-to-bottom club, with Guy, Hayter and Wellens scoring the goals. The home club actually led at half-time, but the

second half was dominated by the Rovers and three good goals resulted. The only fly in the ointment was a bad ankle injury for Heffernan. On the following Tuesday was the FA Cup first-round replay against Oldham Athletic at the Keepmoat Stadium. Mark McCammon replaced the injured Paul Heffernan and Martin Woods came in for Mark Wilson, who had also taken a knock at Port Vale. McCammon put the Rovers in the lead, but on the stroke of half-time Oldham equalised and four minutes into the second half they went in front. Despite persistent pressure on the Oldham defence, especially after Neal Trotman had been sent off following two bookings on 84 minutes, the Latics held out to claim their place in the next round against Crewe Alexandra the following Saturday. The Rovers, however, were now out of all the Cups and would have a rest on that Saturday and then concentrate on the League. They were in sixth place at the end of November after an unbeaten run of seven League games.

Tuesday 4 December brought a home game against Brighton & Hove Albion and another goalless draw. The two teams were level in every aspect of their record and were only separated for sixth and seventh places by the fact that the Rovers had scored one more goal than Brighton. During the match both teams cancelled each other out so there were few scoring chances. Mark Wilson had replaced the injured Brian Stock in the game against Brighton, but Stock was back for the next game at Oldham Athletic, replacing Mark McCammon, along with Steve Roberts, who came in for the injured Gordon Greer. For the fourth time in six weeks the two clubs met, but this time in the League, and a penalty by Hayter in the last minute of normal time rescued a point for the Rovers. Eight days on, the Rovers perennial bogey team, Yeovil Town, visited the Keepmoat and, as usual, went away with the three points from a 2–1 victory. The Rovers fielded the same team for the second successive match. A rather fortuitous goal for the visitors came in the first half when Darren Way's shot, covered by Sullivan, hit Steve Roberts's foot and cannoned away from the 'keeper and into the net. Twelve minutes from time Marcus Stewart made it 2–0, but in the 90th minute of normal time he was sent off after two bookings. In a last, desperate effort to get something from the game, the Rovers got a consolation goal when Terry Skiverton put the ball into his own net. Thus, Rovers' unbeaten League run ended. The last Saturday before Christmas, 22 December, took the Rovers to Crewe Alexandra. The manager made three changes to the starting line up, bringing in James Coppinger for Martin Woods, Paul Green for Mark Wilson and Jason Price for Lewis Guy, in a match that was so one-sided it was a wonder the score wasn't doubled. The Rovers played some scintillating football against a team who gradually buckled under the pressure, resulting in Gary Roberts being sent off after 77 minutes for two bookings. Price scored twice, five minutes either side of the interval, but it wasn't until the last minute of normal time that Green added a third. Two minutes into added-on time, Guy put the final touch to the scoreline. Boxing Day, a Wednesday, brought Northampton Town to the Keepmoat and provided the Rovers with three more points following a win by two clear goals, both scored inside the first half hour, by McCammon, who had come in for Hayter, and Lockwood. The last match of 2007 came on Saturday 29 December at home to Southend United, who were two places and one point below the Rovers, and it resulted in another win, 3–1. Gareth Roberts replaced Sean McDaid, who had suffered a hamstring injury. Lockwood injured his upper arm or shoulder in the first minute and was off the field for several minutes receiving treatment. He returned to the pitch in time to take his place for a corner and was in the right place to head in the first goal after seven minutes. Southend equalised some 10 minutes later, but Green put the Rovers in

front on the half-hour mark, and a volley from Gareth Roberts following a corner three minutes before half-time gave the Rovers a third goal. This win put the Rovers into fourth place in the table at the end of the year.

The new year began with a visit to Walsall on New Year's Day, a Tuesday, with James Hayter coming into the starting line up and Mark McCammon dropping to the bench. Walsall were just a point behind the Rovers as a result of an unbeaten run of 14 games. In added time at the end of the first half Price put the Rovers in front, but the home team responded in the second half and equalised on 73 minutes to get a 1–1 draw, a fair result on the day. The Rovers had a free weekend after this game because their scheduled opponents for Saturday, Bristol Rovers, were still involved in the FA Cup. So the next match was a home game against second-in-the-table Carlisle United a week later. McCammon and Hayter switched places for this game, but it was substitute Hayter who provided the difference between the teams when he scored the only goal of the game seven minutes from time after a cracking game of football as it should be played. The build-up then began for the contest at Leeds United, a game everyone had been looking forward to, and over 3,000 Rovers fans swelled the attendance to 31,402, the second-highest attendance in the Division at this stage of the season. An unchanged Rovers team had no qualms about going out in front of the partisan crowd and playing their brand of football. After 21 minutes a free-kick to the Rovers just outside the penalty area was rifled into the Leeds net by Stock for the only goal of a good, hard game. Leeds fought to get back on level terms, but the Rovers matched them all the way. The following Friday, however, the Rovers came down to earth with a real thump. A 4–0 drubbing by Swansea City certainly avenged their defeat at the Liberty Stadium, but their task was made easier when the Rovers were down to 10 men after Steve Roberts was sent off for a professional foul after 58 minutes.

However, the Rovers were already two goals down when that happened, and two more goals late in the game only put a shine on it for the Swans.

The Rovers were still in fourth place as they went into the next game at home to Hartlepool United four days later. Matt Mills came in for the suspended Steve Roberts and Mark Wilson replaced Martin Woods. A goal in each half from Wellens and Lockwood gave the Rovers the victory that took them into second place, but still 10 points behind the leaders Swansea City. On the last day of the January transfer window two players were brought to the club to strengthen their push for promotion. Gareth Taylor was signed from Tranmere Rovers and Stuart Elliott joined on loan from Hull City until the end of the season.

Into February and the next three games were won with four clean sheets in succession. Steve Roberts was back in at the expense of Matt Mills and Brian Stock replaced Mark Wilson for the first game of this trilogy on Saturday 2 February. This was a visit to the Lions' Den, where the Rovers completely overwhelmed the home team and blasted three goals into the Millwall net, firstly by Price, just before half-time, then Coppinger, with a thunderous drive from 25 yards after 77 minutes, and finally Green in added time. A week later Matt Mills replaced Adam Lockwood, who had a groin injury. Bristol Rovers visited the Keepmoat Stadium for the first time and went away protesting about the two penalties awarded to Rovers in the second half. Stock scored the first after 64 minutes and substitute Heffernan put the second one away deep into added time. The same line up played at Bournemouth three days later, with two goals from Price securing the points. The eagerly awaited return game against Leeds United was due on 16 February in front of a sell-out attendance, but a heavy overnight frost on the uncovered pitch left it frozen and unplayable for the noon kick-off. Recriminations were soon flying around, but the club have no responsibility for the

maintenance of the pitch – it rests with the stadium authorities. The last game in February was against fellow promotion candidates Carlisle United. A hard-fought, excellent game of football was decided when Danny Graham lost his marker and met a cross at the near post to slot in for the only goal five minutes from half-time. This loss saw the Rovers drop down a place, but only on goal difference behind Nottingham Forest. Carlisle were one point behind, but the battle for the coveted second place and automatic promotion would rest with these three clubs.

For the first fortnight in March the team were required to play twice a week: Saturday at Tranmere Rovers, Tuesday at Bristol Rovers, Saturday at home to Port Vale and Tuesday at home to Gillingham. All four games were won, but injuries once again began to take their toll proving the value of having a big squad. Tranmere were in the last Play-off place after an unbeaten run of nine games and were four points behind the Rovers, but Rovers took the lead in the second minute with a tremendous strike from Coppinger into the top corner from just outside the penalty area. This set up a tremendous battle, with the Rovers under the cosh for periods of the game, but a tremendous defensive display meant they kept a clean sheet and took the three points, which put them back in second place. The downside was that Price received an ankle injury. At the Memorial Stadium in Bristol Paul Heffernan came in for Price and immediately made his mark when Coppinger set him up to volley home from just inside the penalty area after two minutes. This precipitated a battle that got rather scrappy and heated at times in the second half, but again the Rovers kept a clean sheet. Against Port Vale, two goals from Heffernan and McCammon in the first 18 minutes set the Rovers on their way, but a defensive slip let Vale pull one back just past the half-hour mark. While the visitors tried hard to get something from the game, the Rovers defence was in no mood to give away any more goals. An unchanged team achieved the same result against Gillingham when goals from Coppinger after four minutes and a penalty from Heffernan two minutes into the second half were enough to take the points, despite a fight back by the Gills, who scored on 56 minutes. The Rovers had now narrowed the gap between them and Swansea City, who seemed to have hit a dip in form, to six points, and visions of becoming champions were beginning to emerge, but two more away games followed that soon put such thoughts to bed. A visit to the Withdean Stadium at Brighton produced an even game, with a controversial penalty being the deciding factor. Sean McDaid came into the starting line up for Mark Wilson. Stock hit the bar early in the game, but other chances for both sides were few. On 56 minutes Stock was adjudged to have brought down Forster in the penalty area and was booked for his protests. The decision looked harsh from the sidelines, but it stood. Forster took the kick, which Sullivan saved, only for the Brighton player to net from the follow-up. The following Friday, Good Friday, saw a visit to Yeovil Town for an afternoon kick-off. James O'Connor made his re-appearance in the team, replacing Paul Green at right-back. Green took over in midfield from Sean McDaid, who dropped to the bench, and Stuart Elliott made his first start, replacing Mark McCammon, who joined McDaid on the bench. A blustery wind and occasional rain made it hard going, but Yeovil were soon on the goal standard when Skiverton headed in after 22 minutes. Nine minutes later they went two goals up when Sullivan came out of his area to field a long ball out of the Yeovil defence. Owusu chased it down as Sullivan controlled the ball, tried to dribble round the Yeovil player, lost the ball to Owusu, who then had the simple task of hitting into an empty net from 25 yards. While the Rovers were not out of the game, they only found the net on 73 minutes when Heffernan rifled in. In the final 15 minutes the Yeovil defence

were under tremendous pressure and three bookings represented their desire to keep the Rovers out. They did just that, the three points taking them further away from the relegation zone. Easter Monday brought Oldham Athletic to the Keepmoat Stadium, and for the fifth time in the season the two clubs faced each other. The Rovers made two changes, with Steve Roberts coming in for James O'Connor and Mark McCammon replacing Stuart Elliott, who was on international duty with Northern Ireland. Steve Roberts and Brian Stock had been selected for the Welsh squad but had received dispensation to play in this game. The Rovers, who were third after Saturday's games, three points behind Carlisle United but six in front of Nottingham Forest, badly needed points to keep in touch with Carlisle. However, they could only manage one point from a 1–1 draw while Carlisle went five points in front. Heffernan put the Rovers in front after 37 minutes, but Oldham fought back and levelled in the 52nd minute. Although the Rovers tried hard and had chances as the game ran down to the final whistle, they couldn't make the breakthrough as the snow came down to provide a Christmas card picture. This was 24 March, and it was supposed to be spring! The following Friday evening saw a crunch game at home to Nottingham Forest. For the Rovers, James O'Connor came in for Steve Roberts and Jason Price replaced the injured Mark McCammon. Playing some good football, the home team had the majority of play but could only muster a single goal from a terrific free-kick after 74 minutes by Gareth Roberts a couple of yards outside the penalty area to the right of goal. His left footer hit the inside of the near post and bounced in, giving the Rovers the goal that divided the teams at the end of the game. As Carlisle only drew on the following day the Rovers were back to three points adrift of them. Forest had dropped below Southend United into fifth place, nine points behind the Rovers.

On Tuesday 1 April Leeds United were in town before a full house at the Keepmoat Stadium. An unchanged Rovers squad turned out against a team struggling to get into the Play-off places. The Rovers once again dominated the game with their football, but despite their majority of possession they still lost the game to a goal out of the blue after 20 minutes when Alan Sheehan rifled in a free-kick from 25 yards. The Leeds defence was pounded in the second half but still held firm, with 'keeper Casper Ankergren in fine form. Adam Lockwood suffered a badly cut foot early in the game and would be out for some time. So for the next match at Huddersfield Town Steve Roberts came in for the injured captain and Brian Stock took over the captain's armband. The Rovers had a bad start when they went behind to a goal from Williams after six minutes and were definitely second best in the first half. The two strikers, Price and Heffernan, seemingly got the blame and were replaced five minutes from half-time by Gareth Taylor and Mark McCammon. The move paid off seven minutes into the second half when Taylor shot in after good work by Green, but with the Rovers threatening to take over the game they were pulled up short on 59 minutes when Mills was adjudged to have brought down Brandon as he ran clear on goal. Mills was sent off and Holdsworth put the Town back in front from the free-kick, just outside the area. With their backs to the wall the Rovers defence saw off the Town's attempt to make their numerical advantage count, and then six minutes from time Coppinger fed Green, who went on to hit a terrific drive into the home net and give the Rovers a point. The Rovers were still in third place but were five points behind Carlisle United and only four points in front of Nottingham Forest. Another Friday evening game on 11 April brought Swindon Town to the Keepmoat Stadium. The manager had to make a number of changes and gave Sam Hird his first League start of the season, in place of the suspended Mills, Lewis Guy came in for Coppinger, who went down with a virus mid-week, Sean McDaid replaced Wellens, who was suffering from back trouble, and Gareth Taylor and Mark McCammon started the game after replacing Price and Heffernan at Huddersfield. The Rovers did enough to win the game, with goals from McDaid five minutes before the break and a penalty converted by Stock halfway through the second half, after McCammon had been brought down and Aljofree was sent off for the offence. The following day Carlisle United lost at Leeds United, but Nottingham Forest won at Tranmere Rovers. So Swansea City were top with 86 points from 43 games and were sure of promotion to the Championship, while Carlisle United and the Rovers were certain of a Play-off place. The following Saturday the Rovers visited Leyton Orient, whose hopes of a Play-off place had vanished after five successive losses, but they didn't let their recent record keep them from giving the Rovers a good game. Orient took the lead after 45 minutes when Wayne Gray headed in a cross from the left. McCammon equalised for the Rovers on the hour mark, and a competitive game ended all square at a goal apiece. Swansea City lost at home to Yeovil Town but were still crowned champions because Carlisle United had lost at home to Southend United. Nottingham Forest won at home to Luton Town and Leeds United took the points at Millwall, so the League positions remained the same. The penultimate game for the Rovers was at home to Luton Town, who were in last place and already relegated after a very troubled season in which they had been deducted 10 points. Although Luton made a game of it, there was never any doubt about the Rovers being in charge, and goals by Mills in the first half and McCammon late in the game gave them the three points. The Rovers were now in second place, one point in front of Carlisle United, who had lost at Millwall and dropped to fourth place on goal difference, while Nottingham Forest took the third position after winning at Hartlepool

United. Southend United lost at Tranmere Rovers but stayed in fifth place, with Leeds United in sixth place after winning at Yeovil Town on Friday evening. With one game to go, the top six teams were now known, but not the final order.

The day of reckoning arrived and Rovers knew what their task was. They were in second place, one point in front of Nottingham Forest, their only real opposition because of their overwhelming goal difference over Carlisle United. A draw was no good – only a win would see them promoted to the Championship automatically. The Rovers were to play Cheltenham Town away and Forest played Yeovil Town at home. The Rovers had a battle on their hands because their opponents they had to win to save themselves from relegation to League Two. News soon came through that Forest were leading 2–1 after 20 minutes, while Rovers' game was goalless, but that changed after 24 minutes when Cheltenham took the lead through Steve Gillespie. Then came news that Forest had scored again and were 3–1 up as the Rovers battled to get on equal terms. They came out in the second half determined to get the necessary result, but effort after effort either went wide or it produced a good save from goalkeeper Shane Higgs. The Rovers totally dominated the second half and drew level on 76 minutes when Green latched on to a flick-on by Price and lashed his shot into the net. Still they poured forward, but the defence of the home team and the magnificence of their 'keeper kept them out. A rare attack by the home team led to a corner, which was played back to Keogh, who crossed to the six-yard box, where Connor got the touch to push it past Sullivan into the net and put them in front, completely against the run of play. The ground was rocking with the intense excitement of the home crowd, while the Rovers fans, over 1,500 of them, watched in disbelief. The team tried hard to put things right in the remaining time, but Higgs foiled them yet again. Time ran out, and while the home crowd celebrated staying in League One the Rovers learnt that Forest had won and would take the automatic promotion place. Carlisle United drew at home to Bournemouth and equalled Rovers' points total but had an inferior goal difference so were in fourth, Leeds United beat Gillingham at Elland Road and leap-frogged Southend United – who could only draw at home to Port Vale – into fifth place by virtue of a vastly superior goal difference. These positions meant that Doncaster Rovers would play Southend United and Carlisle United would take on Leeds United.

The blow of letting automatic promotion slip through their fingers hit the players so hard that they held a meeting and resolved to rectify matters. The first match was at Roots Hall on Friday evening, 9 May, in front of the Sky Sports cameras. The Rovers boss made three changes, Lewis Guy for Richie Wellens, out with back trouble, Jason Price for Gareth Taylor and Paul Heffernan for Mark McCammon. A hard-fought game ensued, but it ended as it had begun – goalless. However, Heffernan spoiled the night when he flicked his head into Mulgrew's face and received his marching orders just two minutes from the end of normal time. This meant a three-match ban and he'd be out of the second leg and the Final if they got there. So it was all to play for a week later at the Keepmoat Stadium, again shown live on Sky Sports. This time the watching audience would be treated to a right royal goal feast, and some good football to go with it. The winners already knew that they would play Leeds United at Wembley after they had beaten Carlisle United on aggregate. The Rovers started well and were awarded a penalty after 10 minutes when Price was brought down. Stock put it away and the Rovers were up and running. Price made it two on 20 minutes and Coppinger added a third in the 39th minute after cutting inside from the right and shooting hard and low into the net from the edge of the penalty area.

Four minutes into the second half, Coppinger made it 4–0 when he ghosted past three defenders before rifling in from 20 yards. Ten minutes from time Coppinger completed his hat-trick with the best goal of the night. He took a free-kick on the right of the goal just outside the penalty area, played a 1–2 with Green before curling the ball into the top corner of the net to set the seal on a great win which took the club to Wembley. Bailey scored a consolation goal for Southend two minutes from the end of normal time and the team had played a full part in the game by never giving up, while their travelling supporters in the 13,000 crowd never stopped singing.

And so to Wembley, on Sunday 25 May, for the first-ever all-Yorkshire Play-off Final in front of an attendance of 75,132, which was the biggest live crowd that a Rovers team had ever played in front of. There were also millions watching live on Sky Sports. The stadium was magnificent, with the pitch in great condition, there was a fantastic crowd and it was a fabulous occasion. All the Rovers fans wanted to see now was their team do what no other Rovers team had done for exactly 50 years – to win and take the club back to the second tier of English football. Five years earlier Leeds United were in the Premier League and UEFA Cup, while Doncaster Rovers were in the Conference, a gap of three divisions, and now they were in the same division and playing each other at Wembley. John Ryan had a dream 10 years ago when he took over the club he has supported all his life – to get them back to where he thought they belonged. At Wembley he saw that dream come true.

The Rovers line up for the biggest game of their lives was: Neil Sullivan; James O'Connor, Matt Mills, Sam Hird, Gareth Roberts; James Coppinger, Paul Green, Brian Stock, Richie Wellens; Jason Price, James Hayter. Substitutes were – Lewis Guy for Coppinger 86mins, Mark McCammon for Wellens 72mins, Adam Lockwood for Price 80mins. Gareth Taylor and Ben Smith were not used.

The Rovers set the tempo from the word go and could well have been in front in the first 20 minutes, as they carved open the Leeds defence time after time with some brilliant football. However, heroics from the Leeds goalkeeper, Casper Ankergren, with four fine saves from Coppinger and Hayter, saved Leeds. Gradually the West Yorkshire team came into it and even play followed to the break. The turning point of the game came two minutes into the second half. Stock swung a corner into the penalty area for an unmarked Hayter to bullet a header past an astonished goalkeeper. The Rovers continued to play their brand of football but were gradually pushed on to the defensive as Leeds set out to redress the balance. Leeds spurned the few chances they had, and a terrific display from the Rovers defence in the last quarter of the game meant that Hayter's goal would take them all the way to the Championship. It was time to celebrate for the Rovers as their fans took over Wembley.

This terrific match was a great advert for football in the divisions below the Premier League. John Ryan has to be thanked for overseeing the renaissance of this famous old club, together with the club president Trevor Milton and his fellow directors. The manager Sean O'Driscoll, his assistant Richard O'Kelly and their backroom staff have been the architects who have shown the players the way to go, and the players are the ones who have put it into practice. Then there are the fans. Without the fans there is no club, and there are thousands who have backed Doncaster Rovers through the lean times and feared that it would disappear 10 years ago, but they stood tall as the club progressed over the succeeding years and saw their wildest dreams come true.

SETTING OFF

Sean O'Driscoll takes the driving seat.

Jason Price shares a joke with Gareth Roberts.

Fans wait for the players while Doddy sets his directions.

Doddy takes over.

Coppinger gets ready for Mario Kart.

Ready to go.

Gareth on his DS!

Away we go.

Thumbs up from Spike Lee.

Relaxing.

Graeme Lee and Paul Heffernan.

Sully takes a snap.

Looking around.

Richie shares a laugh.

A pensive Brian Stock.

James O'Connor and Mark Wilson.

Trying out the changing room.

James Coppinger and Craig Nelthorpe.

Steve Uttley takes a photograph of Wembly Way.

The fans arrive.

Wembly Way.

More fans arrive...

...and their coaches line up.

Stretching the legs.

We are Rovers.

Big Bananas.

Irish Rovers.

Follow us.

The admin staff on the road.

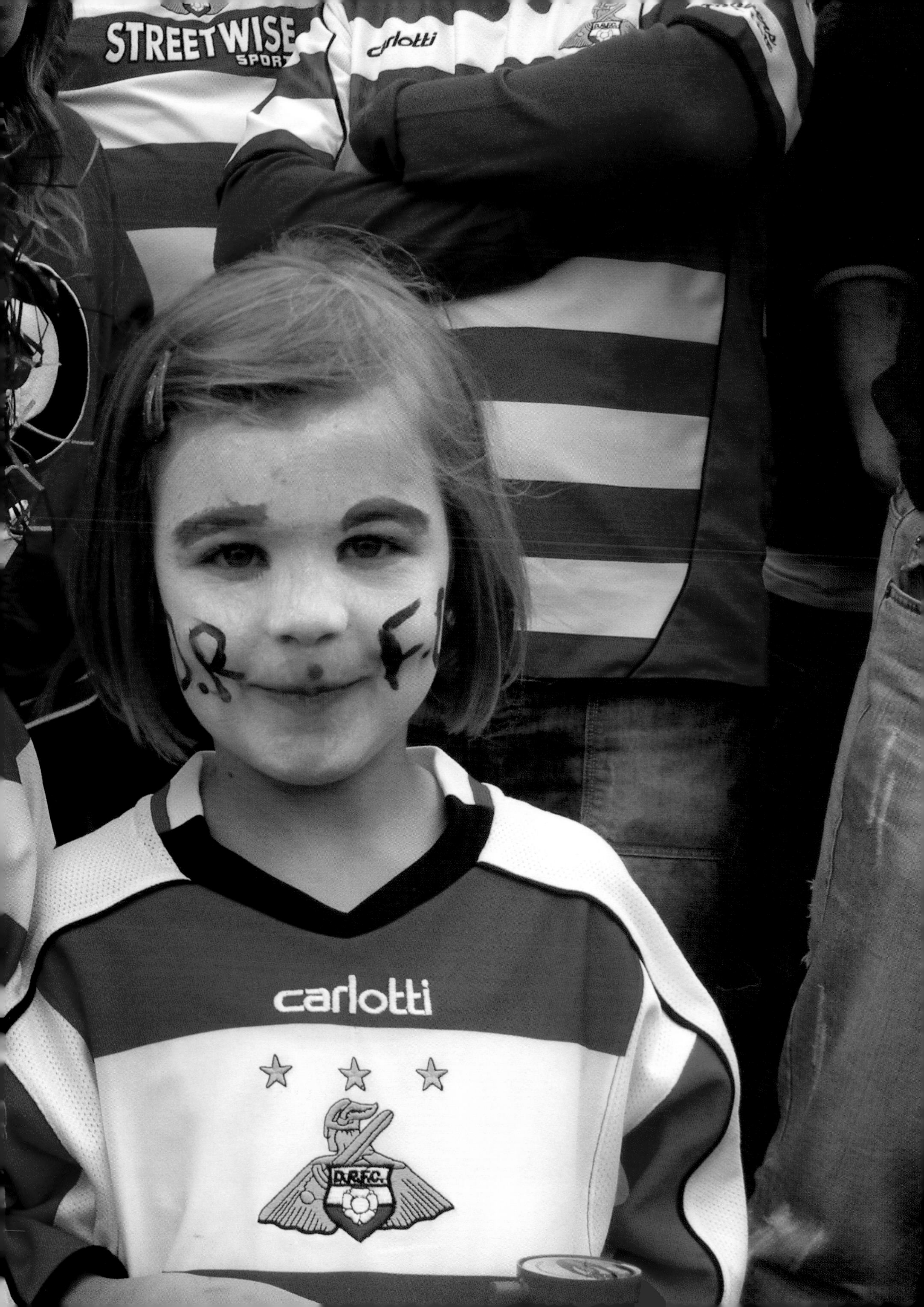

STREETWISE
SPORT
carlotti
carlotti
D.R.F.C.

Bring it on.

Reds line up and the spirits are high.

The fans are all kitted out and ready for the match.

Young and ready.

Three generations.

Thumbs up.

The Alisons are ready.

Flags are up.

The lottery gang.

The Community Fans.

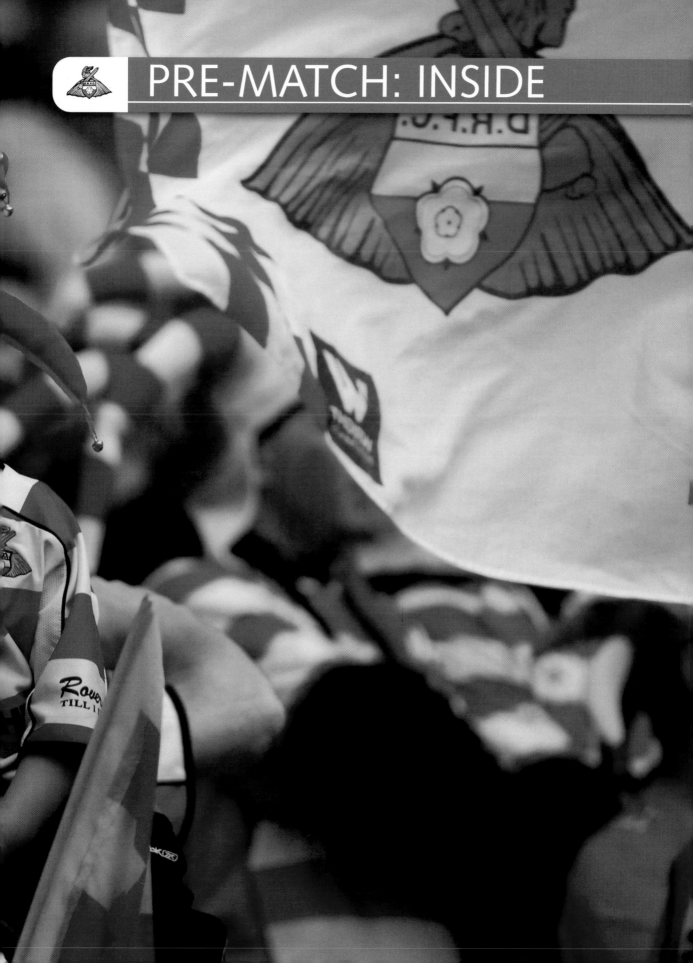

The flags fly.

Donny Dog and Denise Pickersgill.

Welcome to Wembley.

The noise echoes around the stadium.

'Where 'R' 'U".

Everyone is on edge.

Two tribes go to war.

'Barmy Army'.

All smiles.

Raring to go.

All we care about is DRFC.

So proud.

Behind the goal is a sea of red and white.

George gets ready.

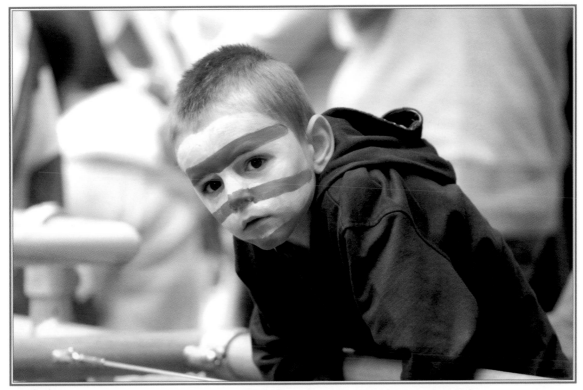

Painted up.

What a crowd!

Ready to start.

Make some noise.

Sean O'Driscoll leads the team out.

Coming out of the tunnel – tension is building.

Through the smoke, the players arrive.

Lining up.

The national anthem.

The scoreboard.

Leeds – but Red!

Rovers till we die.

Jason Price.

James O'Connor.

James Coppinger.

James Hayter.

Sam Hird.

Jason Price.

Rovers' biggest-ever crowd.

Pride of Yorkshire.

James Hayter.

James Coppinger.

Paul Green.

Jason Price.

The fans sing on as the action continues.

James Coppinger.

James Hayter.

Brian Stock.

The support is overwhelming.

Paul Green.

Richie Wellens.

I can't sit.

Reds at the back.

Goal!

Celebration time.

I scored!

Total delight.

Goal!

We are going up.

Celebration time.

Happy!

Final-whistle madness.

All join in.

Commiserations.

BBC Sheffield's Alan Oxley interviews Matt Mills.

We are there – Neil Sullivan.

Mark McCammon and Brian Stock.

Paul Green.

Matt Mills.

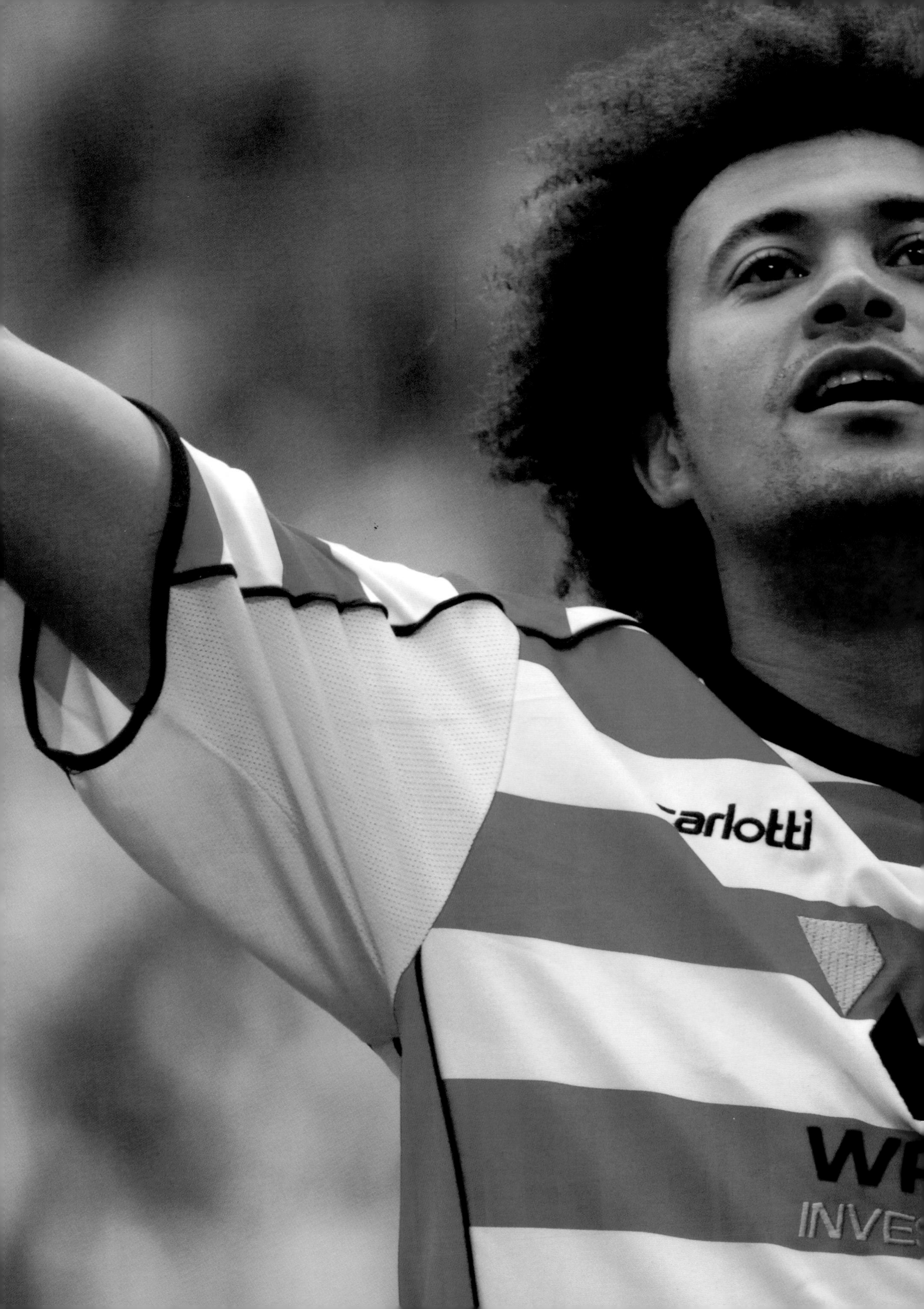
arlotti
INVES

We are going up.

Flag on.

Magic moment.

Sky get in on the act.

Total delirium.

Stock and Green.

James Coppinger and Jason Price.

In front of the fans.

Sky interview Brian Stock.

The doctor watches on.

Pure ecstasy.

Going up for the Cup.

North Branch on tour.

Through the Leeds fans.

The Board celebrate.

Brian Stock leads his players.

Ready for the trophy.

We are up.

Brian Stock and Adam Lockwood.

Pass it along.

Photo - PA Sport

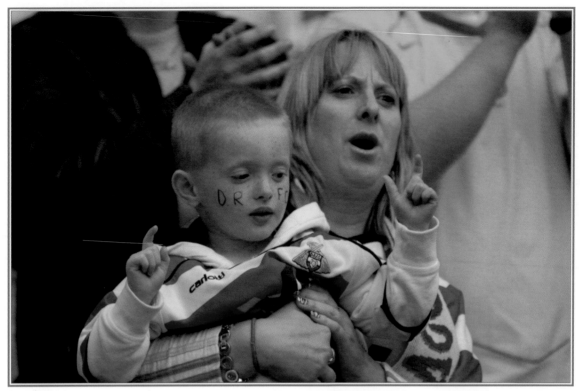

Family joy.

Sing up.

We have made it.

Pass it on...

...we all want to hold it.

James O'Connor.

Gareth Taylor.

Mark McCammon.

Another cheer.

We can't believe it!

Emotion.

Waiting to give the bottles.

Jim Brieley gets soaked.

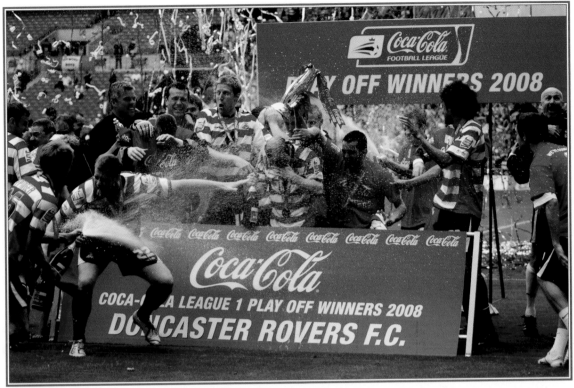

Sprayed.

Matt Mills and James Coppinger dance.

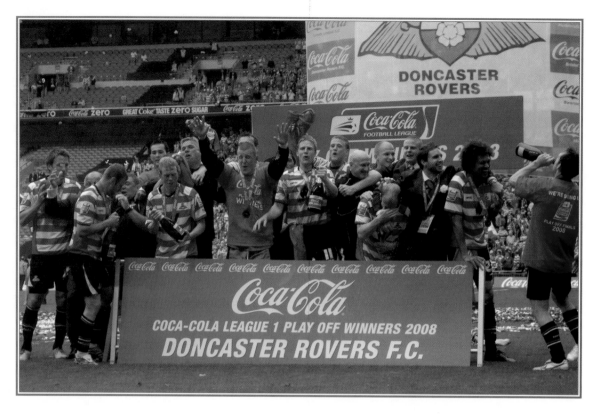

Champagne time.

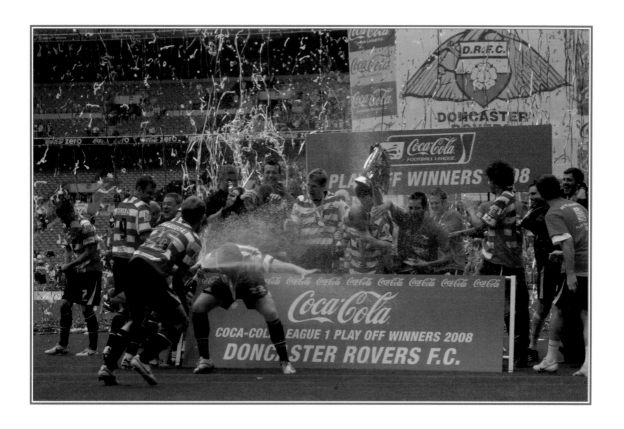

Party time.

Richard O'Kelly talks to Coppinger.

John Ryan holds up the Cup.

Kitman Dave Richards.

Sean O'Driscoll with the Cup.

Stuart Highfield and Phil Ryan.

John and Lynne Ryan.

Chairman's delight.

I see you.

Goal scorer Hayter.

Richard O'Kelly.

Gareth Roberts.

Matt Mills.

Paul Heffernan.

Covered in ribbons.

Sam Hird.

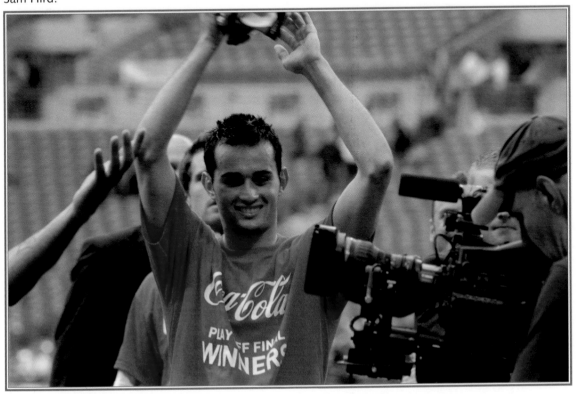

Jason Price.

Price hugs Matt Mills.

Running and diving.

James O'Connor and Matt Mills.

James Coppinger and Richie Wellens.

Neil Sullivan and Ben Smith.

James O'Connor and James Hayter.

Matt Mills.

Paul Green.

Brian Stock.

Jason Price.

Adam Lockwood.

Sam Hird.

Gareth Roberts.

The rovers fans are in Heaven.

Neil Sullivan being interviewed.

Greg Whelan interviews John Ryan.

'Don't spoil my suit!' John Ryan gets covered.

Celebration time with a beer or two.

The chairman joins in.

Ben Smith dances.

Matt has a beer.

A proud captian – Brian Stock.

All together now.

Calming down – the kitman checks the beer.

Lined up.

Next to the satellite truck.

On the top.

James Coppinger holds up the Cup.

Moving through.

Pricey claps the fans.

From the top.

We love you.

We are going up.

Piggy back.

No flagging.

Magic flag.

Donny Dog!

Mrs Robinson's famous scarf.

Viking warrior.

On my shoulders.

Happy.

Fun all the way.

Sean on the balcony.

John Ryan and Dick Watson.

Mayor Martin Winter, Sean O'Driscoll and Jack Ryan.

Paul Heffernan, James Hayter and Lewis Guy.

The Ryan brothers, John and Phil.

Dick Walton, Sean O'Driscoll and John Ryan.

Relaxing.

John Ryan's speech.

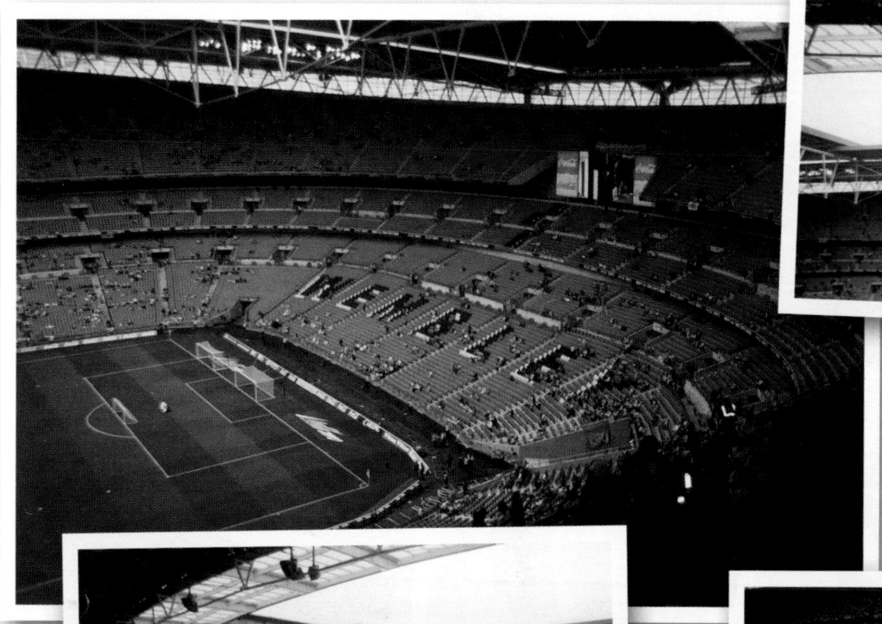

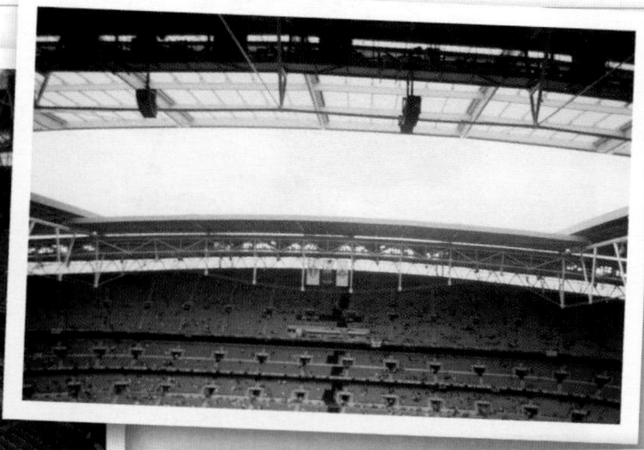

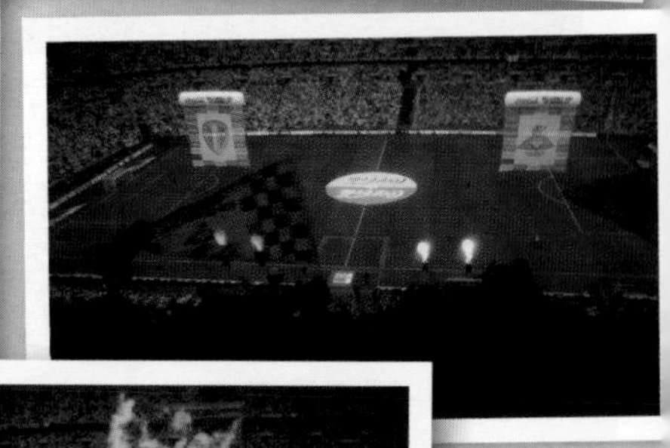

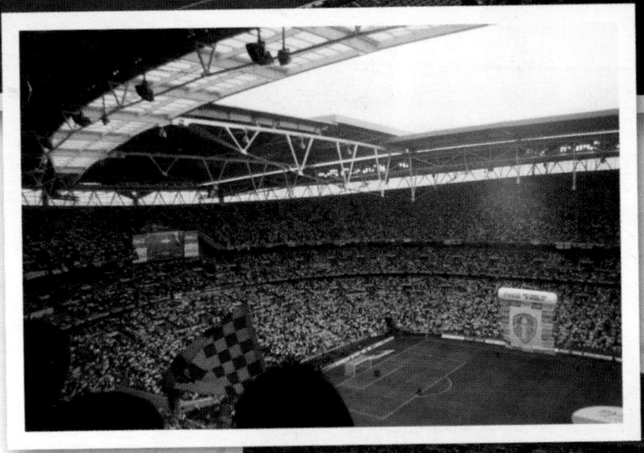

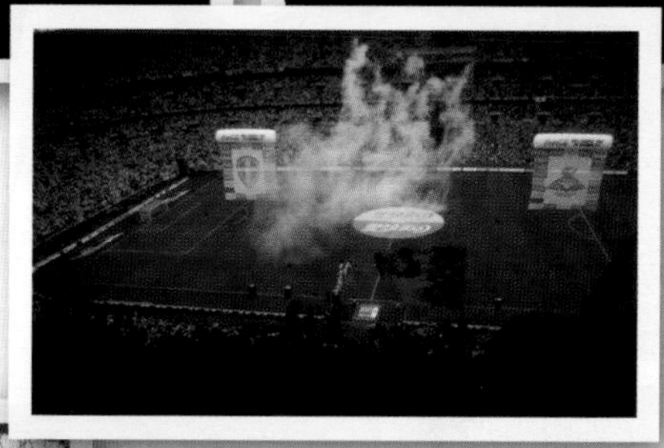

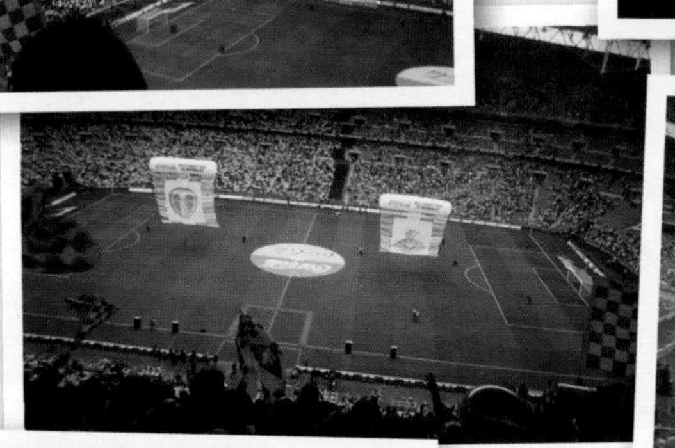

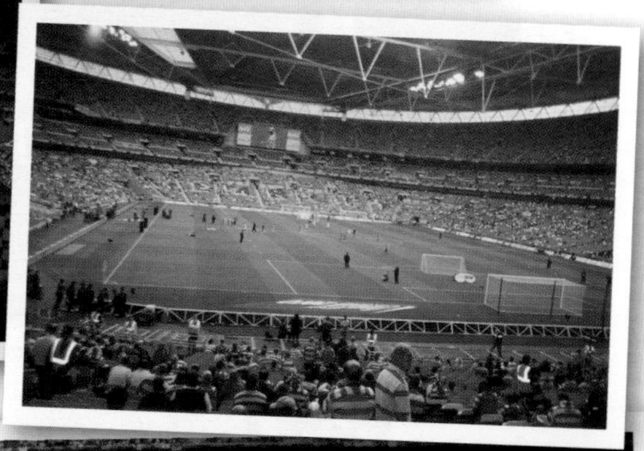

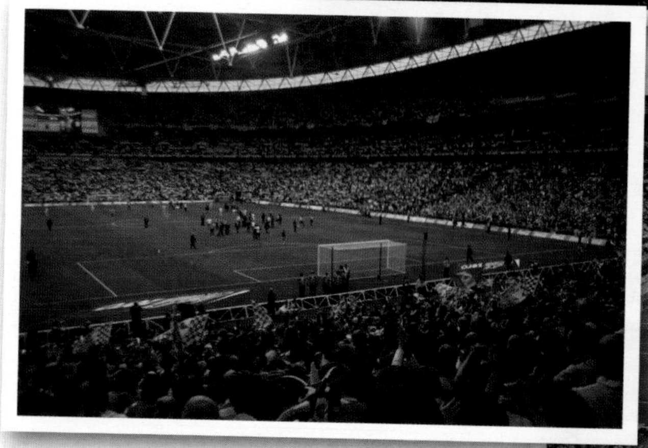

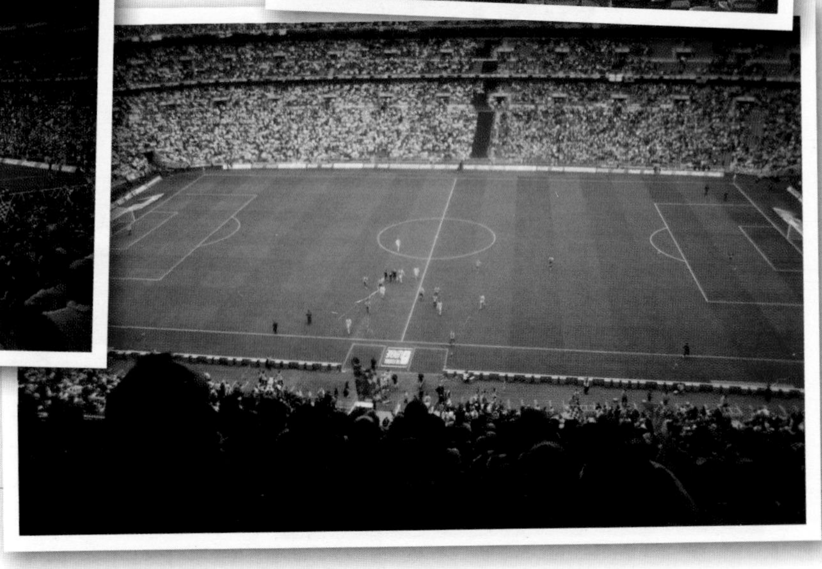

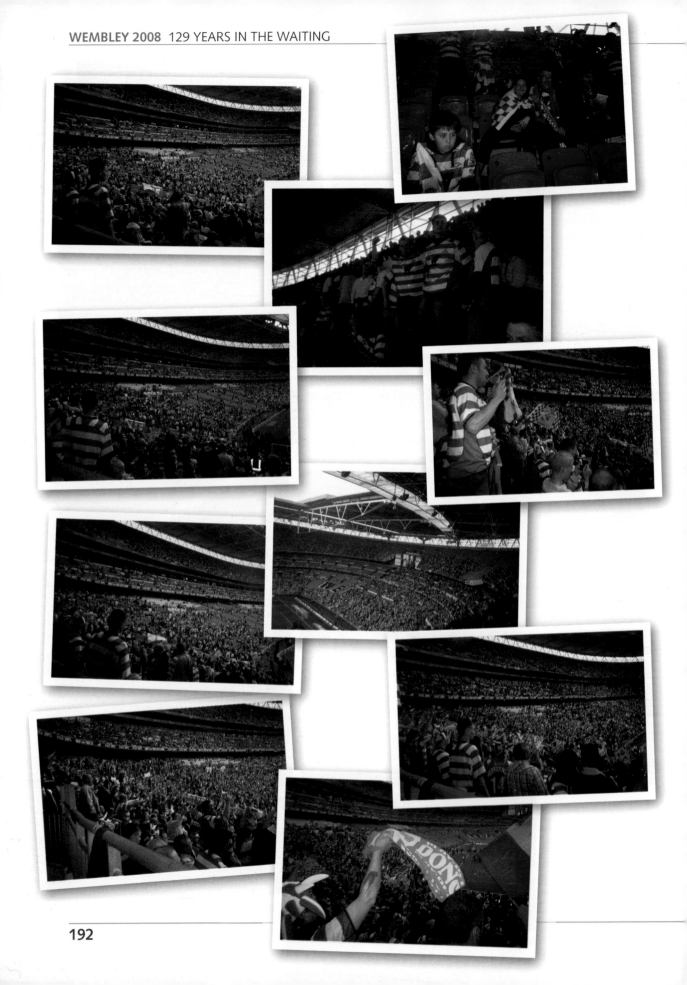